Destroying Angel

Wesleyan New Poets

Destroying Angel

Nancy Eimers

Wesleyan University Press

Published by University Press of New England

Hanover and London

Wesleyan University Press
Published by University Press of New England, Hanover,
NH 03755
©1991 by Nancy Eimers
Printed in the United States of America
2 3 4 5
CIP data appear at the end of the book

Some of these poems appeared, sometimes in different
versions, in *Antioch Review, Crazyhorse, CutBank,
Gulf Coast, In Art, Indiana Review, The Nation,
New Voices, North American Review, Passages
North, Quarterly West, Sonora Review,* and
Western Humanities Review.

"Where We Came From, Where We Are Going"
draws upon material from Michihiko Hachiya's
Hiroshima Diary and John Hersey's *Hiroshima.*

I would like to thank the MacDowell Colony and the
National Endowment for the Arts for their generous support.
I am also grateful for help and encouragement from
Susan Prospere, Rich Lyons, and Leah Giniusz.

for Bill Olsen

I wish twas plainer, Loo,
the anguish in this world.
I wish one could be sure
the suffering had a
loving side.

Emily Dickinson, letter

Contents

I

The Gypsy Moth   3

Migrations   5

Training Films, Nevada, 1953   7

Where We Came From,
    Where We Are Going   8

Even the Dead Can't Sleep   15

Magnolia Season   17

II

Basic Treatments   23

Robbery   25

Bad Love   27

Edith Frank   28

Aslant   30

Black Angel   31

In the Hour That Doesn't Exist   32

No Friends of the Heart   35

III

Liars   39

Another Kimono   40

A Visit to Amherst   42

The End of the Season   44

Out of the Soul   45

Photograph of Strasbourg   47

The First Photographer   49

Fourth of July   50

Fiery Dust   52

I

The Gypsy Moth

On invisible thread the scalloped worm
is almost lost to the world
of finished things—corrugated oak trees
just across the street, a swollen Pacer
no one seems to own, though it is your hand
holding the curve of the bumper, forgetting.

Disturbed by breath, the slightest green
wafts in and out of shadows
taking it wholly or leaving it
alone as it swings in our faces,
a flicker hard to see
apart from spring, the day around it:
its accordion pull and release
is so slow it seems aimless. Magnified,
its clumsiness might be the graceful

first steps into flight,
though now it is hitching its body pointlessly
toward the lowest branch, still inches
away. In another week the tree will begin
its dying, given leaf by leaf
to the difference between itself and sleep,
which is wings. Clouds film over the sun
and blow over the private

inner white. We don't say
we already miss it, somehow knowing not to,
knowing each other better for idle talk.
The lines cross our faces more finely
each year—what we hope
is a complication, not of touch but the little

we love beyond possession. The trees let go
of the sky almost effortlessly,
rain on our shoulders and hair, soaking us
back into ourselves, where we can imagine the fineness
of each other's discomfort, how close
to common air.

Migrations

Instinct drives monarch butterflies west to a certain tree
where their eastbound parents lit
for the first and only time, and instinct keeps egrets
in the reeds in places where freeways lift
and cars pass over the marshlands.
This freeway's bottleneck slowing the traffic
is a big brown mutt lying sideways
with its legs stuck stiffly and peacefully out.
Its nose and muzzle are red. It is finished—
one quick swerve of grief
and each lane of cars straightens out
and runs smoothly away from the mess.
Our turn to pass, we are getting ready to look down
and feel whatever it is we can wrest
from the nervous swoop of beginning a day
when a white ungainly bird flies over the cars
like somebody's clean white fluttering slip
run rampant, or the soul of the dead dog
shocked into flight by our grounded
weak little hurry. Ungainly egret,
far from the lowland rivers spilled into meadows,
where long carded grasses rush on without moving,
and the snowy plumes of the egret move on
over foreneck and back but never rush.

So these cars part briefly
for islands of stranded women and children, for mufflers,
for bricks dropped from open-backed trucks,
and sometimes for a dead dog
if it still looks enough like a dog
to suggest its running or playing might wake again.

Sometimes the flat wet side of a reed is a flash of white,
or a rising egret is partly veiled
by its own white, flustered glare—then it drops
behind the fence of green.
That whole world's elusive to humans.
You have to accept this,
parking in sodden weeds, stepping down blindly in
                    ankle-deep mud
that deepens and sucks off one of your shoes
before giving sudden way to the freshwater pond
where red-black mullets swim close to the surface.
When you throw a rock you can part them,
but herding them back together,
random and jittery inkspots,
takes patience that brings on courtliness
to the egret approaching its nesting mate with
                    slow deep bows
in the slowed-down time that patience takes,
though now you've got to go,
commit yourself to that flowing north or south
                    you came from,
packed tight in the stream with other glimmers.

Training Films, Nevada, 1953

When the pigs squealed away from the noise,
which was everywhere, and the blast,
which was down in the ground and high in the air,
and the heat, which was tearing around
inside them, we were looking down
from the helicopter and trying to hold
the camera steady. All along we'd been worried
about the younger kids—that, trying to see,
they'd stick their necks out of the trenches
and get a red-hot eyeful, or get scared and run
before it was safe to be out and running.
The sergeant had *ahemed* and written three words
on the blackboard, *noise, heat, blast,*
and said, boys, if you're close enough to be risking
blindness or sterility, you'll be killed anyway
by the heat or the flying glass. And I saw
these two kids sneak a look at each other,
not as innocent now. I thought of the little Bikini Islanders
chanting a native version of "You Are My Sunshine"
in the training films. The pig we called Control
was safe and sound in his little pit,
but the others were running everywhere,
bumping into each other, making that awful sound
that I think is only terror, pure, unmixed with embarrassment.
We didn't know the sound would follow us
long after we'd pulled away into the air.
Later that day, when things were quiet again,
they threw the pigs in the back of a truck.
A few were still moving around and moaning,
so I took the butt of my rifle to one,
having been taught not to pity
an animal being slaughtered,
or it will die hard.

Where We Came From, Where We Are Going

1. Pale Skin

In the intimate territory of sidewalks
where we were free with our secrets,
she showed me a tiny, toothpick-spoked umbrella
which opened and gave us a tiny Japan,
pagodas, a string of round, red paper lanterns,
and two black-haired girls in yellow kimonos.
We opened and closed it so often it tore.
The paper ring at the nexus of toothpicks
unpeeled in a long strip of newsprint
whose bent, black letters unscrolled in a line.
On the other side was part of someone's face—
the lips and half of the nose.
It seemed those black, straight lips
were the mouth of Japan
about to speak out their sacred and terrible message,
concerning the two of us
and our lives at the very moment we stood there,
silent and scared on the sidewalk in front of our two houses,
on Wayne Drive, one block from Forest School
and a half-block from the forest preserve,
where hoodlums made you eat cigarettes
if you whispered about them,
insinuating themselves from the trees and the shadow.
We looked around for the nearest adult—
Mrs. Dettmer, clipping the vines on her trellis.
She explained about parasols,
how the rain would shrivel them,
but, in sunlight, they shaded the faces and arms of the women,
who believed a pale skin was beautiful—
then we ran back out to play,
scorning those other girls for hiding their faces,
afraid they might burn in the sun
like paper in fire.

2. In the Ruins of the Fukuya Department Store

Light still travels from east to west,
from the city to the hills. We called the clusters of smaller bombs
flower baskets. What opened inside us that morning
was more like one huge flower of light,
and the light, like the darkness, cannot be helped,
as now a child picking bluets and Spanish bayonets in the ruins
cannot help feeling responsible for their beauty,
then thinks to himself, Oh well.
Too bad. It can't be helped,
and tucks them inside a sleeve
and away from the sky.

3. Pale Flowers

On the skin of some women,
the burns had made patterns of flowers
from the flowered material of their kimonos,
dark flowers conducting heat to the skin
and deserting the background white,
deserting whatever pale flowers were left
in the scorched and curling silk.
And the men wore flash-burn undershirts
and suspenders across their naked chests.
Those who by miracle or coincidence
had not been hurt were ashamed:
"Excuse me for having no burden
like yours," and the rubble-buried ones
screamed back formally, "Help, if you please!"
The eyes of soldiers caught looking up
for the first shy glimpse of this morning's *B-san*
had melted and streaked down their faces,
as if, having witnessed the bath
of a radiant goddess, they must not see
her shame, her terrible shame
has left everyone naked.

4. Envelopes Full of Ashes

Water beads on the back of a silkworm
crawling across my house, having the impact
of small, weak things on a larger world
after violence. Rain still drips
from the leaves, and frailty rears up
and brandishes its tiny front feet,
then falls lightly into the wet grass.
There seems to be no harm done:
it undulates onto a grass blade
and rotates its blunt, green, shiny head
as if restoring a fallen order.
I think it a shabby trick
the way memory offers a single image
in place of life—
the tree flowing back to its roots
is gone, the rest of the house,
the afternoon, all gone,
the faces, my wife's and my son's—
even now I reduce things to images,
as if disaster were nothing
more than a simplified peace.
Now that there is time for leisure,
hospital workers have piled up wood
from the fallen houses and lit a fire.
They lay the bodies down,
burning them one by one to keep
the ashes separate. Only a handful
goes into each envelope with a name
typed neatly across it. A small boy cries

when a bird blunders delicately
into the flames, drops down, and smolders
bright red, then red, then gray.
He stops crying. He has already learned
how to simplify grief—
that a handful of feathers and air
is a handful of ashes.

5. Fires

Some nights the only light
was the glowing fires of the dead.
For days no one knew what had happened
but everyone tried to guess: incendiary bombs,
gasoline poured out of airplanes,
poison gas, some new, incredible bomb
that would go on killing for more than seventy years.
Because life was simple and terrible
after the white flash, people evacuated
in single file, holding their arms out in front of them
to keep the burnt flesh from chafing.
On some, the skin hung in fluttering strips.
When asked, at the outlying villages,
where they had come from, where they were going,
the few who would speak murmured only, *this way, that way,*
pointing toward Hiroshima and then toward Miyajima,
the Sacred Island, whose camphorwood torii
stood in the distance like an empty bird roost.
Whatever spirit abides in wood
must fly at the first breath of fire,
but a man must live in the burning house
of his body, and carry its hot breath,
and breathe it on each cool leaf
he fits, strawlike, between his lips
for its scant beads of water.
He must kiss its coolness
however it hurts
when the leaf grows warm.

6. The Blue Star

The Chinese character for doctor
means *comforter*. This morning
I pulled out a clump of my hair,
and all around me the other patients
are searching their bodies for skin spots.
This twisting and turning opens
wounds, and an old man cries, "It hurts!"
I am sure the doctor who pats his hand
is losing hair. After the first shock
of politeness wore off,
there were jokes about diarrhea
and wrangling over the army supplies.
Some of the other girls were complaining
because the big army boots had all been issued
to men. Everyone uses his khaki-
colored life preserver as a pillow,
and there are plenty of flags—
red and white signal flags
the children wave, running up and down
between our mats, and old Mrs. Saeki
uses the rest for dishcloths and towels.
From the last box the doctor
brought me a white bowl with a blue star
in the center—it taught me
to think about leaving
this life, though some long afternoons
when I'm mixed up from morphine
I think with so many dying
the star is too small to receive us.

Even the Dead Can't Sleep

At dusk the field slacked off
and slid away under the dark,
but light winged in and out
the branches creaking down the street:
corner woods that were paltry
in daytime, when kids walked dogs
one end to the other, shrinking
red blobs of windbreakers,
fur-ball dogs bouncing sideways
and skirting the sudden, rickety house
that lived there alone
with a couple of thickset Harleys
braced against each other. A center
for each of us neighborhood kids
to remember, our brief returning
thought a monument to our fear of it
even in daylit hours,
that house that drew back
to its little window, a radiance
by the time our fathers got home
and home pulled strongly the other way.
Then we sat deep in plump-backed chairs
in our different houses and watched cartoons:
sniggering animals chasing each other
through tunnellike houses, running on air
to the bicker of snare drums
past the same old table, flowerpot,
window that hovered together,
slid away, and returned with a promise:
that terror was commonplace.

We were safe, we knew we were safe,
but how could any one of our houses hold
its soft bonging of kitchen pans
away from the tired roars of the Harleys
just waking off in the woods?
I would wake in the middle of night
and start thinking, everyone's snores interrupting,
ignoring each other and something larger
behind them went on and on.
A girl in the high school
had died in a car crash, and the death-smell
seeped through the car, they said,
and wouldn't die. They rested
the wheels against cinder blocks
in her parents' backyard. That's why
some things last an eternity
too long, I thought, I still think
even the dead can't sleep as deeply,
as recklessly as the living.

Magnolia Season

Therefore all seasons shall be sweet to thee.

—Coleridge

This morning a wind bears the sweet and sulky
odors of marriage and makes a mystery
out of little passions and pets.
An eyelet slip like simplicity's wedding dress
shimmies low on a clothesline
slung between trees, and hands
bang down the lid on a garbage can
in the distance, hands more awake
than my thought groping towards them,
hands whose opening blankness lets go
as this morning's blossoms let go powerfully
and yet withhold a greater light.
Each flower split wide and disarming
desire by offering everything,
birds flying in and holding still on the leaves
while Mexican girls wait under the tree.
They are waiting for a bus to come
or for boys, for whatever sweeps them along
the bright, hot day. In the breathless
meantime they hold each other's arms
like fallen petals, loved with an absolute
inattention, as they are free to love,
their arms not yet full
of babies and groceries, babies and laundry,
girls not yet the young mothers I see at bus stops
waiting, legs hugged tight by children
whose black, stoical eyes will offer
their generous absences to just anyone.
I have no daughter or son,
and the morning offers its sleepy promise

it may not remember to keep:
that its sweetness will multiply.
I wish you were here with me, right now,
though I know we can't always share things
even by talking about them—
whatever the one says well or even perfectly
the other buys and is, in silence, immune to.
Silence nods off in the yards,
Queen Anne's lace and chicory louder in silence
than nearby traffic, whose silvery *whoosh*
lifts monumentally over the trees
but can't quite let go. Silence
never lets go of us: nameless lovers
in the movie *Hiroshima, Mon Amour*
held on through the early hours,
we watched them stroking each other
with their terrible patience, as if hands
were the light now working its glitter of dust
into the infinite traceries in the skin,
or the shadow, now smoothing it over.
Their love is an argument
between memory and forgetting,
and it goes on and on in whispers
while the movie goes back to 1945,
year whose dazzled survivors lie
perfectly still because everything hurts.
And one boy stares awesomely back,
his lips torn off, his teeth growing raggedly
out of his jaw: whatever his eyes say
keeps to itself. Meanwhile, the lovers marry
every touch to its absence,
though none of us knows how this happens.

And now, when your parents tell you
they are moving back home to Nebraska,
with the world in such a mess,
not even sure they want grandchildren,
in the wonder that flows out of pity
you tell me *I feel that we're paying*
for someone else's happiness.
Maybe the most we can plan for
is loneliness, from which we have already borrowed
abundantly. If over us the great oaks shoulder together
to ward off some terrible thought,
maybe their ancient quiet will comfort us.
And if what makes the world
a terrible place for kids is the little
maybe, no wonder
we live in it vague and unpestering,
each one looking away from the other
because it is restful to lose him
and find him again at the edge
of vision, where teacups wait to shatter
and breath is a small rash promise
made over and over again to a vast
joy beyond consolation.

II

Basic Treatments

If a soldier felt hot two hundred years ago
and developed a rapid pulse
at the thought of love,

the army physician tied tape at the wrist,
held his hand by the fingers and stretched
so gently they both were moved.

Then he pierced the vein longitudinally
so the impure blood could escape,
though for some men the purity was too powerful

and the body died.
A hundred years after that, in another war,
a surgeon could cut off a wounded arm or leg in
                    seventeen seconds

with instruments crabbed and childish now;
then his hands would have nothing to do
with the pain blooming out to the shape of the missing
                    fingers and toes.

Then his hands would lie quietly
to the next hands they touched
as if anyone's hands could ever die out of the mind.

No. Memory is a little museum of miscalculation and
                    haste.
And the fatal errors of voodoo and pharmacy
have turned quaint in New Orleans' Vieux Carré,

where three red globes in the pharmacy window
once warned travelers there was plague in the city,
so breathe into your hands and go back to the river

until you see one red globe, one green, and one yellow
that will mean the mystery of the preparations inside
can soothe again the restless spirit though not the body,

will mean crushed ice and rock salt once more cool the
                mineral waters
transformed by the faucets to nectar soda,
will mean there are throat syrups laced with heroin,

gout tablets the size of horse pills,
Dr. Otto's Nerve and Bone Liniment serving both man
                and beast,
sick feeders, cupping and bleeding devices,

and when rose-fever or love is no longer
enough of a mystery,
there beside lesser potions marked Lucky and Separations,

there is the viscid cap of the shiny destroying angel,
mushroom whose white touch will stick to your hands
and you'll feel yourself float back over the river

leaving someone to stand there in ecstasy,
face tilted up to the show globes,
bright wasted moment your hands understand

about as much as they understand wanting.

Robbery

Here had been an untangling
while we swam *there,* wind blowing waves into big hands
pushing and pulling us,
hands so cold the fingers won't work
like a comb through a ripple of hair
or pick up a single handkerchief from a drawer
so they hold us in handfuls.
At home the kitten curls up on a pair of clean socks,
seamlessly sleeping, whatever it might have seen
now a part of the fitfulness of the curtains
blown halfway out the open window,
and lying so limply across the couch
are red and black stereo wires, uncrossed, attached to nothing
as if something hugely explosive and delicate
had been dismantled and taken away
by someone who stepped carefully out the window,
but first he must have gone upstairs,
we speculate, in the jittery spell
that presides over moments of absolute precision,
to browse through the closets and drawers,
where panic has flung itself headlong on the floor
in a crumple of jeans and underwear and my blue,
          half-opened umbrella,
the empty top drawer of an empty dresser
a little bit open and leaking,
the Canon AE-1 still there inside the green backpack zipped up tight,
those teeth closed over a secret
so simple and powerful that some young kid in a hurry must open it
and then close it again without looking inside,
run down the stairs without the vial of Xanax I left on a table

(whose calm will rush over you without making you too sleepy),
go straight to the red and black tangle that makes perfect sense
when the fingers are all calmed down
to hold the wires they promise
can no longer meet
in a house this quiet.

Bad Love

for my sister

In the middle of nowhere
any kind of love is better than no love—
thoughts of your asshole boyfriend,
the waitress who told us to come back soon,

the voice of some trucker wanting a blow job real bad
from any white man traveling north,
static answering in and through and around
the long silence flying south.

At the scenic overlook it was twilight
but down in the trees it was already dark
and the salt lick was barely blue—
if we cupped our hands to it

we would feel them turning cold.
Some deer were browsing there,
moving awkwardly in the grass
as if wearing high heels,

clumsy as high-strung things are when they come to rest,
then running away
with little white flourishes of their tails,
bad love rushing after good

and you, watching it go
inside you standing there perfectly still.

Edith Frank

Why should we wait until we've reached a suitable age?
Why should we bother?
—Anne Frank, *Diary*

What gets me by is the art of living,
scouring the already-rotten potatoes and carrots,

quiet mornings that look like scenes from Vermeer,
reading, sewing, petting the cat, arresting peace in each small,
          hermetic industry.

Yesterday Miep saw an ancient, terrified Jewess parked on a stoop
by some Germans in a long black car that meant waiting

was almost over—her eyes flicking full-speed between her future
          and past.
I tell my daughters how lucky they are,

but my youngest, Anne, believes the everydayness of things
has a truer version we have to invent,

that though fresh air and sunlight are done with us for the time,
we have not even started with them. Impatience restores her

as coffee used to restore me, unspiralling spirits
bearing me up in the morning, sometimes too high—

I'd hear my voice bend like a loop of wire
into intricate shapes. There hasn't been real coffee for months,

but she still has her all-absorbing moods, her pictures of film stars,
the Dutch royal lines she traces in neat, blue, sprouting trees

that lift her delicately from her body for a while,
which lately is bursting out of its ragged clothes.

And out of all this comes whatever happens
between her and the Van Daans' son in the attic's eternal night—

despite what her father and I have to say to her.
(Despite what he and I say to each other in bed.)

She thinks I don't know these things
happen without consent, without family or friends,

these things begin and end in loneliness.
Let her have this new love. I said it aloud,

and Otto, thinking me bitter or cold, turned into the dark
where he lay very still and waited, where gladly

I followed him to others lying awake,
listening in a dark no longer private.

Aslant

The sun was way to one side,
and light passed over Bean Blossom down in the
          trees somewhere,
spilling a little on hilltops that swelled and got in the way.
The rest of it fell on fruits and vegetables,
long brown boards of the roadside stand.
The tomatoes looked warm,
so I cupped my hand around one
and took it up and down the rows with me.
My mother's arm bent around clusters of bittersweet
she wanted to buy me; my father was stalking
          the outside tables
of Indian corn studded brick-red, black, and yellow.
Each so intent I wanted to push away,
for the long day we'd spent in the country

seemed helpless with us still inside it,
just sitting around while the lake waves staggered
          into each other.
Had one of us said something, anything,
we'd have steered that old man back down the
          wobbly path
and away, and out of our picnic. He came
as someone lonely always comes,
asked on by any little silence
that won't tell how to discriminate between sighs,
blown leaves, our moving lips.
The smear of light on his wrist, when he held it up
          to show us,
flared into points—his gold retirement watch
like another sun overflowing, deserting itself
for homesick, obedient us.

Black Angel

You can see her across the graveyard,
not rising but sinking to earth
and hulking there, just above the headstones.
Almost spread, her wings are caught
mid-flare, one breath behind
a lift into corrosive air.
From beneath her, we stare straight up
where trees are a delicate afterthought,
the little green furls and fissures
all branches dwindle to in spring.

But she is as pure a shock
as the sky's primary, finished blue
that pulls away from her in all directions.
She turned black years ago—
one night for grief or faithfulness
with the patient instinct of chemicals,
copper and oxygen, toward something
more gradual than white.
Her eyes are simple,
un-irised, as if her sight had failed
at specifics: how formal and serious
we are, the wrinkles in my shorts,
your ruffling tiers of hair.

The afternoon stalls,
wanting to see as barely
over headstones, driveways, hills
of houses groping down to ours
until each disappears for love,
any one thing we close our eyes
not to forget.

In the Hour That Doesn't Exist

By the time she graduated from high school, Ethel Greenglass
(Rosenberg) had almost never been outside the Lower East Side,
eaten in a restaurant, or ridden in a car.
                                                    Ilene Philipson

She might have been one of those girls not buying anything,
not buying the look of a basket with slats all busted through

or the apples not heaped up but stacked, precisely,
            so every bruise showed
I was honest. The ones bruised all over I put on top.

My hand would be sick of the shape of them,
            sick of the cold, hard skin—
in that year of surplus apples everywhere

there were more of us apple sellers, I thought, than wares,
pressed together, jostling, running all over the streets

or, like me, chased deep into themselves like the black trees
whose silences have a way of hanging back.

Grand little silences telling you *please don't stare.*
I didn't find hers out then, or what it was saying in the sad, empty
            voices

of 1930, year slept away in an empty reservoir we called Hoover Valley,
1931, year they opened the Waldorf-Astoria in Manhattan

and finished the Empire State, tallest building in the world—
how could I? The silly girls clung to each other,

floating arm-in-arm down Rivington, swinging their feet
        on the fire escape
as if our poor day below had nothing to do with them,

pushcarts, snow coating over the apples, gray snow, apples,
blown sheets of that day's rumpling, forgettable history—

not those girls! pretending the one right, whispered indifference
would heal all things, tumbling down into so many golden hands.

As if they could ward off these sweet loud apples with words.
I just glared right through them.

It's only the present in me that can focus,
brave her, apart from the others, falling back, turning—
        does she see me?—

wrapping a raincoat around her dress to lie down in the street
with the strike squads of women I once joined, blocking 36th street.

Thrilled. Just lying there. Breathing a sky of exhaust.
Tonight she was in all the papers again, for the last time—

how smoke curled out of her head toward the skylight and hung there.
They thought it unwomanly. That she died a lot harder

than other girls, or her husband minutes earlier.
That the spirit is risen or dead

but the soft, dark body can hunger on—for what?
To eat out in a restaurant? Drive through the Lower East Side
        with her friends?

Be touched by a man? Or never, never in this or any world
to be touched again. I would like to have seen her

and spoken to her, to rub my hands on hers like snow on snow
while the winds bump together and roll around in our heads.

See, once you look you can never look away.
So, hot June night, I am looking everywhere

as your heat searches all around her remembering drift and fall:
where are the apples? and the hands fall open,

marrying desire to its pure and childish body.

No Friends of the Heart

Believing the heart was the center of knowledge,
the ancient Egyptians would leave it inside the
            mummified body
and hope the other organs, bottled and placed near the
            catafalque,
might be put to some more enlightened use.
The summer I worked in a factory
I was told by Edelmira to stay in college
to learn more wonderful stories
and teach them to others.
I would say we were almost friends,
working across the table from each other,
oiling and polishing notebook binders and stacking boxes
all day, every day
in a white fluorescent eternity.
By midafternoon the women from Cuba and Puerto
            Rico and Mexico
had made each other lonely
by talking in Spanish too intimately,
parents, husbands, children, brothers, sisters,
names that went by and imagined the rest,
all the details that get so homesick
we can't stay long with each other's lives.
But when Edelmira was generous with my future,
imagining a white room with windows
and the sound of my voice addressing itself
to a classroom's shy and receptive silences,
she was leaving herself in the dingy present,
the little table with somebody else across from her,
the piles of binders, ring after ring after ring
that would not meet. When I tried to be cheerful—
you have so many friends here—

she answered, putting her hand on her chest,
no friends of the heart.
She said it in English and it sounded true,
breaking out of her language and into mine
with the urgency that has still not learned
to be indirect.
If there is another life,
I hope it is ruled by affection,
which in this life we can only restore to each other
unexpectedly, a chance bit of news, an odor,
an old, bleak feeling just biding its time.
It seems in this life the heart is not yet the center
             of knowledge,
but we have always been in awe of blood.
When I sat by the pond with you a few days ago
you said one reason to have a child
is so lovers can dwell at last in a single body.
But friends can't live in each other's bodies.
If sometimes language fails them
less than their looking quietly at each other,
if vocalizations, gestures, expressions
are meaningless layers we have to cut through somehow,
I don't know what we will find inside.
For now, all we can do is take care of each other
from the outside,
as when mosquitoes swirled up from the grass
and we brushed them off each other's arms and
             faces and hair.

III

Liars

Aunt Peace died in bed with a rose
   in each cheek, and a snow-white braid
      down her back, and a smile that belonged

to the angels. She was safe and cherished,
   as I was, a *dear reader* lying in bed before breakfast
      on Sunday morning, faded Plenty,

her sister, tending her for the last time,
   closing her eyes with coins
      that would multiply and pave her way to heaven.

She kissed her lips in the courtly way
   they used to have toward the infirm,
      the elderly, and the gentle distressed,

who no longer had the advantages we have.
   That same morning, as I lay in bed reading,
      my grandmother died in a hospital in Chicago.

She was holding a cup of coffee and saying something
   to the nurse when her heart stopped,
      just like that. She dropped the cup

and was gone, and in a similar clumsiness
   my grandfather had trouble dialing the phone,
      so the doctor called us. I told my brother

to shut his mouth, she wasn't dead,
   and slammed the bathroom door in his face.
      That night my grandmother whispered to me in my bed

but the nurse said to pay no attention,
   she wasn't really there, and that
      having lied about that, she might say anything.

Another Kimono

So many poems with kimonos
opening darkly. Drifting over us
from the blackest corners
of touch and kiss. Kimonos
our bodies aren't worthy of
until bodies are shed
like a mottled skin that hurts
when we peel it off.
Whichever broken birdcage
my father saw clean through,
Hiroshima or Nagasaki, he
isn't too sure anymore, and you
can't hear even one wave
lap into his voice that sailed
too quietly over the ocean
and home again. You can't hear
what went into the looking
more and more finely
that rubble seldom teaches us
how to stop. How to see
each glint without wondering
what larger brightness it must have
belonged to. Each flame
on the back of the dragon
was larger and sillier
than its red tiny marvelous
angry stitches. So he bought
a black silk robe instead
and brought it home to my mother
along with his sailor hat
and a green mottled box
with a white silk lining

and rows of Japanese characters
like dancers with too many broken
arms and legs. Inside
its foreignness there was
nothing. Did she put the robe
on when they touched,
small flames burning everywhere
to forget the bitter cold
sunny afternoon, did they lie
down together and take off
everything but the bare trees
with bark dull and black
like a shining
turned in on itself?

A Visit to Amherst

From the dead who are not
                        our own
I feel sadness and love
are borrowing us for an afternoon,
their old stones
                    sugar-coated,
wearing away
in the slow rain—
                    dust,
names and dates, dissolving
wings.
            You say *lead the way,*
but where
            after this profusion?

Stone flowers scattered heavily
                            on a baby's grave
were the parents' "small consolation,"
each petal hard and contained—
    now the parents are buried behind her
in what seems to me just a blur
                            of the years they survived.

But as a parent you mourn every one of them,
and when your 13-year-old son
                            frightens you sometimes
    into pity
by holding your hand openly in the street,
you are dazzled that grief
                            has so light a touch.
The woman we came here to see
                            had been small and light
as a child
and her name on the white stone
    looked commonplace,

but only a few graves were inside the iron fence.
The white slabs struck at me—

how every death
                    is like a child's
whose poignance we can't get right.

And I feel like your child
                    when you buy me an ice cream
and tell me to take my time
while you talk of your favorite daughter,
                              your teenager Katie,
chasing you all around the house
                    for your package of cigarettes.
You ditched it
          and then let her catch you,
falling all over each other
   for the game was an old one
you both had to play in a hurry
                    before you forgot it.

Emily Dickinson lived here
   and now she is dead.
In her room where death seemed huge
                         by comparison
I was grateful for small things,
   the names of your daughters and son,
   the lines on your face,
the modest stone that stands at the fence
                         like a child.

The End of the Season

Today on the sports page two boys wear basketball nets
        around their necks,
as if happiness were that artless,
not like the winning slam dunk that was prepared for
half a court back, the forward's thigh muscles lunging
grotesquely with every stride
torn out of the not-quite-finished last. The forward
        explained,
"I went out there and played."
He doesn't think about it, but we believe
a man can fly, or that he can hang there a minute
on grace alone and not be pitied,
though we pity the things that have to come back down,
what else is there to do?
In southwest Houston, a man with time on his hands
built a bus stop to look like a tiny Victorian house
and kept adding ornaments—stained glass windows,
        an armoire,
two dark-webbed antique mirrors,
and, finally, his own white velvet loveseat,
on which people spread newspapers before sitting,
matter-of-fact, like the faithful who stripped the sheets from
        their beds
when St. Cecilia was dying,
dipping the cloth in her blood, that river
no realistic thought in this world could staunch.

Out of the Soul

Field of long grass with a shy, pink side
wind has to coax out of green
                            into being
like Shelley's "soul out of my soul."
   You want to speak
words more familiar to you
                            than your life

an invisible hand petting the grass
in the palm of your hand the feeling
   that watches
                  so open it feels like falling.

You wish your lover were here
                        who would understand
your hand on his face
who loves you for being
                        inarticulate.

No one will ever know
                  what you mean.

When you make love
you both get out of your souls
                        you let them go
to each other
like the pages of books
                  whose kisses
are words glancing off each other.

Your hands on each other's bodies
                              trying to remember
the old words,
then love brims over
                    into exhaustion.

Then you lie together as if long grass
   blew over your heads
a third soul already passing away
                              before you can know it

blowing away through the grass
   toward a time you were by yourself
and something touched you and you blushed.

In the meantime you lie there
                         not talking,
you remember the first time you were quiet
                                        together.
And your palms have that careworn feeling
   the wind blows through them
up out of the grass.

Photograph of Strasbourg

Waiting for something to break
this crowded city, the housetops slant up
toward Strasbourg's only cathedral.
It rises against a sky
so flimsy it's hard to believe,
a held breath. What is wanted
may happen down one of these streets,
even on this street where nothing changes,
nothing dares to move.

In the daytime I don't understand
this hope—the shapes of my neighborhood
shift so easily from shadow to shadow.
No stars or streetlights, but passersby
always looking into my yard
for what uncomplicates them, the silver
edges, objects that answer every time,
the blue Galaxie at the curb
becoming more real than the thought,
night. I believe it as I do science,
or as I believe that down the street
some TV is tuned to baseball,
that the center fielder moves
beyond the range of the camera
as if afraid he were in a play.

Out on the lawn I talk with Lynn
about miracles we'd like to have witnessed:
the shroud of Turin, the face of Christ
in the scorch marks of a tortilla,

Mary in a Yaqui schoolhouse window,
her blue tones of brooding
no workman can scrub away
and so each goes home, relieved
at a drifting in his head,
a vague constellation light-years away.
Talking too much, we're both sad
at thoughts rising like Piranesi's towers,
each delicate pillar extending
deeper, higher into nothingness
until we no longer imagine it.

The First Photographer

Nothing seems far from this imprecision,
a dismantled privacy,
one man's view. The first photographer, idling
at an upstairs window, invented a freedom
he must have loved
even as he loved that back street, the way it resisted
all ownership. Maybe he took one last good look
and perspective became the time light takes
to touch an object incompletely,
without any jealousy: floating in nature,
these images won't quite be fixed.

What he left in these shadows
was not a recognition but a loss
of focus, a moment let go beyond itself
where buildings stretch outside the camera's scope.
I look for a way to feel
about his view, about anything.
Occasionally, a hot stillness drenches my own windowsill,
the blue vase, the small giraffe emerging
clumsily from its mottled wood.

When this moves into that, I try taking it
lightly: if I sit here long enough,
things will start changing. The sun is so careful
not to forget or remember details separately.
Nothing will prevent me from moving
toward another transfigured emotion
I haven't learned yet,
toward all the simplicity I've thought about,
toward my very thoughts,
until exhaustion,
until the moment.

Fourth of July

Forgiving distance
            he said
at least you won't be off on a star.

In the little world
not space but time
hangs over us all

unmoving
            a great haze of light.
Then one night it's gone

like Halley's Comet
that as a child he loved
thinking love was a promise

lifted out of puzzlement
            into amazing doubt:
he saw himself looking up,

a forty-year-old man
and a long-haired star
            still desolate

from its infinite ride.
At the fireworks
I heard another small boy

say the stars
don't have to do their jobs
tonight. A bouquet of green and red fire

died into sparks,
but the sparks weren't ready
            to die

so they floated above us,
Robert, Tony, De,
lots of parents and children

sitting like the embers
of some enormous fire
that had blackened

the earth,
now quiet, now leaping up
                          into wonder.

Whatever these days
                    will be the embers of
I am glad for them.

Glad for a small girl
holding a sparkler away from her face
   then writing her name on air.

I guess we have to be
                      that brave or unthinking
have to disappear

into every day that will take us
farther apart
              have to be in love

with the meantime
burning the end of the sparkler
   showing the darkness is nothing
                              but delicate splinters.

Fiery Dust

Anne Frank whose anger went several layers deep
when she told her diary pages
paper is patient
wrote down things she would have said aloud
if there were no other people living in the world.
Even admitting there could be such loneliness
made her feel free,
so she wrote down more words,
leave me in peace to her nagging parents,
and then, *who knows, the day may come when I'm left alone*
more than I could wish!
The threat of that solitude was almost soothing,
a world without people strangely imaginable,
where what she called "the simple beauty" would wait
in the grass, the fields, and the sky
for someone to come out and look at them all.
And so far she has kept them waiting
here in New Hampshire, where the pines' lanky trunks
have been in a moody light all day,
going green to copper to sheet-metal gray.
In the tiny Secombe family graveyard I watched the trees
turn every chance of our knowing them
into another chance,
but if as Anne Frank believed these woods have life
I have to believe
they may also be mortal.
Every afternoon I sit here, alone and a little silly
to keep a dead family company,
Mary and Sarah, Percy, William and Will
as distant from me as the dead in *Our Town* felt
from their own unappeasable mourning.

Byron once called us *fiery dust.*
He couldn't have guessed what dust would shower down
on the crew of the *Lucky Dragon* out on a fishing trip in
        1954
on a spring day off the Bikini Atoll.
Here in Peterborough in the summer of 1988
I don't know what dust will return to us,
but I hope the woods will remember to wait.
Anne Frank never came back,
but I think it would make her happy
that all of us staying here spend half the day outside,
and at night we play volleyball until dark,
Ralph whose fist wants so badly to fly
that it clobbers the ball
and the ball flies hard right back to the ground,
Jena who sets it up so delicately
you can see its slow revolutions
thinking about whose hands to fall into next,
me, trying so hard to be polite
that I throw myself on the ground when I miss.
The noise we make is not trying to wake the dead
and the ball is not like a sun
we hope we can keep from touching the ground.
We just play because we can't settle down,
and she couldn't either. She wrote until her hand was stiff
while we jump and swat at the ball
and yell as loud as we can.
And the trees behind us
are patient with all that has yet to be said of them.

UNIVERSITY PRESS OF NEW ENGLAND
publishes books under its own imprint and is the publisher
for Brandeis University Press, Brown University Press, Clark
University Press, University of Connecticut, Dartmouth
College, Middlebury College Press, University of New
Hampshire, University of Rhode Island, Tufts University,
University of Vermont, and Wesleyan University Press.

ABOUT THE AUTHOR

Nancy Eimers was a 1987 *Nation* "Discovery" winner and
the recipient of a 1989 NEA grant. Her poems have
appeared in such magazines as *The Nation, North American
Review,* and *Crazyhorse.* She lives in Kalamazoo, Michigan,
and teaches creative writing at Western Michigan University.

Library of Congress Cataloging-in-Publication Data

Eimers, Nancy.
    Destroying Angel / Nancy Eimers. — 1st ed.
        p.   cm. — (Wesleyan poetry)
        ISBN 0-8195-2194-9 (alk. paper). — ISBN 0-8195-1196-X (pbk. :
alk. paper)
        I. Title.   II. Series.
PS3555.I46D4   1991
811'.54 — dc20
                                                    90-50909
                                                    CIP